Lady and Bella's Alphabet Kitchen

A to Z Recipes for Kid Cooks

Written by
ANNETTE BRIDGES

Illustrated by
LESLEY VERNON

Lady and Bella's Alphabet Kitchen
A to Z Recipes for Kid Cooks

© 2015 by Ranch House Press. All rights reserved.

Printed in the United States of America.

www.annettebridges.com

ISBN – 13: 978-0-9976014-5-9

Table of Contents

Parents Love Lady and Bella's Alphabet Kitchen..iv
Acknowledgments..v–vi
Totally Delicious, Totally Friends: Lady and Bella's Secret Ingredient............1
Adorable Animal Crackers..18
Best Blueberry Muffins..20
Cool Cherry Dump Cobbler..22
Delightfully Delicious Doughnut Holes..24
Easy Extraordinary Egg Casserole..26
Fluffy Fabulous Flapjacks...28
Groovy Graham Crackers...30
Horribly Messy Hamburgers..32
Incredible Ice Cream Nanas...34
Jazzy Popcorn Balls..36
Krazy Dog Kebobs..38
Lucky Cheese Log...40
Merry Marshmallow Brownies..42
Nifty Nutty Snowballs..44
Outstanding Orange Drink..46
Pepperoni Pizza Puffs...48
Quick Quiche Cups...50
Rich Crispy Rice Treats...52
Spaghetti in a Skillet...54
Tasty French Toast..56
Upside Down Cupcakes...58
Velvety Mac and Cheese..60
Wacky Wheat Wafers...62
Xcellent Snack MiX...64
Yummy Yogurt Smoothie..66
Zesty Zucchini Chips..68
Cooking Terms Glossary..70
Create Your Own Recipes..74
Meet the Alphabet Kitchen Test Cooks..79

Parents Love *Lady and Bella's Alphabet Kitchen*

"Cooking with my grandson gives us time to bond because we can talk about what we're doing and make some memories together. We love tasting our creations!"
—Judy, Luke's grandmother

"Teaching my ten-year-old son Mack to cook has given him a new feeling of independence. My daughter Ashley loves to make cookies for Grandma after school. She says it's more fun than TV!"
—Heidi, Mack and Ashley's mom

"The joy of filling my kitchen with memories of teaching my daughter to cook warms my heart. Priceless!"
—Dusty, Leighton's mom

"Helping our children learn to cook encourages creativity, self-confidence, and a healthy lifestyle. They may not become culinary protégés, but they'll leave the house knowing how to make more than PB&J!"
—Hollister, Trinity and Holland's mom

"Cooking with my children reminds me of cooking with my mother and grandmother—such a legacy of love baked into the things we make. I know I cherish the recipes I learned to cook with my mom. It's more than good food, it's love!"
—Laura, Chloe and Jack's mom

"Give children the confidence to do one new thing each day and in no time they'll conquer the world."
—Melissa, Cooper's mom

"A one-of-a-kind opportunity! My daughter used her math, measuring, reading, team work, and taste bud skills to create a scrumptious snack!"
—Cynthia, Berghan's mom

Acknowledgments

Perhaps not all cookbooks have an acknowledgments page, but this is not your typical cookbook—at least not to me. Watching the cute television cooking show, *Master Chef Junior*, became the inspiration for *Lady and Bella's Alphabet Kitchen*. My husband and I are big fans. The child contestants not only impress with their cooking skills and savvy, it warms my heart and gives me hope for humanity to see them encourage and cheer for their fellow competitors when they succeed and to see their empathy and tears when their competitors fail. These talented young chefs are my role models in consideration, courtesy, and civility.

Watching the show reminded me of when I taught kindergarten. Cooking with my students every Friday was part of my approach to teaching language arts. Some of the recipes in this cookbook were used in my classroom many years ago. Many more were ones my young daughter loved to make. I wanted this book to feature one recipe for each letter of the alphabet, and I wanted the recipes to be perfect for beginner chefs.

Since the fictional character Lady loves to cook, it seemed only fitting to have an "introduction to cooking" story starring Lady and her best friend Bella. Like their first book, *Lady and Bella: Totally Different, Totally Friends*, this story features spectacular illustrations to color. With a cooking terms glossary, a create-your-own-recipe section, and a photo gallery of recipes by the 26 kid cooks from ten U.S. states and Germany who tested and approved the recipes, this cookbook required a "village" to produce it. Therefore, there are a few folks in the Alphabet Kitchen village I must thank and praise.

My husband John is at the top of my list. It was his wonderfully wise suggestion that I have a team of test cooks try out the recipes. Plus, my book production is only possible because my beloved CFO loves me with all of his heart and supports all of my dreams.

As always, my impeccably smart daughter Jennifer is my biggest cheerleader, whose encouragement I could not live without. I will forever cherish our many fun memories cooking together in the kitchen.

The Alphabet Kitchen Test Cooks were adorable, conscientious, enthusiastic, and meticulous in their cooking tasks. Their grown-up helpers were wonderful and thoughtfully thorough in helping their test cooks honestly review the recipes and give superb suggestions that allowed me to make the directions crystal clear for future kid cooks.

Needless to say this project would not have been possible without my ingenious and brilliant illustrator, Lesley Vernon. She is awesome at reading my mind and turning my ramblings and wishes into a beautiful design.

I am always grateful for my clever and capable editor, Laura Matthews, who has keen eyes and a fervent eraser. She knew exactly how to make my "introduction to cooking" story more intriguing and charming. She is definitely one of my trusted advisors!

Likewise, this book, as with all of my books, has been made perfectly ready for readers and, in this case, future cooks by my insightful and accomplished book producer, Carol Hohle.

I count my blessings as often as I can for the invaluable team of wise women (and one fella!) who have helped my dream as a chick-lit and children's author become a reality. I love you all and sincerely appreciate your role in making my book dreams come true.

Totally delicious, *Totally* friends

Lady and Bella's
Secret Ingredient

Lady wiggled and giggled as she yelped across her yard to her neighbor and best friend Bella. "It's almost time for *Super Chef Doxie Junior* to begin!"

Lady's love for cooking ran a close race with her love for watching cooking shows. *Super Chef Doxie Junior* was her very favorite ever. It was a special cooking show just for kids.

Bella came right over and bounced into the living room with her friend. While she didn't much like to cook, she loved to eat—and Lady cooked some scrumptious goodies. Bella especially loved it when Lady made her delightfully delicious doughnut holes. Dachshunds love doughnut holes because they are round and shaped like a ball—a dachshund's favorite toy.

Lady's dad joined them in the living room while wiping down a plate he'd just cleaned. His job as a restaurant chef inspired Lady's love for cooking. He did most of the cooking at home, too. He always invited Lady to assist him with meal preparation and encouraged her to experiment with creating her own dishes.

The show started with a booming announcement. "The star of our show, Chef Doxter, hereby invites all Doxie Home Cooks to enter a recipe contest!"

Lady's tail started wagging so fast she almost wiggled off the sofa.

"Submit your best recipe in writing along with photographs of the finished dish," the announcer continued. "You will need to prepare your recipe for dachshunds who have never eaten your cooking before and have them fill out recipe review cards. These review cards should be submitted with your recipe and photographs. The winner will be invited to make a special appearance on *Super Chef Doxie Junior* and help judge contestants who will be cooking their winning recipe."

Lady howled, "Oh, Oh, Oh! I want to enter! I would hoot and howl if I could meet Chef Doxter."

"I know the perfect recipe you should submit," Bella cried. "Nobody makes doughnuts as good as yours! Nobody!"

Lady wiggled and giggled at her best friend's idea. But then her wiggles stopped suddenly. She whimpered, "Oh, Bella! I want to, but I don't think my recipe is good enough for Chef Doxter. Besides, sometimes I think you just say

you like my cooking to be nice and not hurt my feelings."

Bella huffed. "I would never do that!"

"What about my eggplant chocolate pizza?"

That had been one of Lady's "experiments." Bella giggled. "Oh, you know that one was wild and crazy. But you are even crazier if you don't think your doughnuts are delightfully delicious. Everyone loves them!" She turned to Lady's father. "Aren't they the greatest?"

"They are!" he said. "And you know how fussy I am. I only like the best." He snapped his towel in Lady's direction.

Lady still looked unsure. Bella remembered all the times her friend had been on the sidelines at her soccer games, cheering her on. Bella wanted to be as good a friend back. She jumped up from her seat and waved her hands in a pom-pom swirl. "Who's the best at cooking? Who's the best cook ever? Gimme an L!"

Laughing, Lady's dad cried, "L!"

"Gimme an A!"

"A!"

By now, Lady was laughing, too.

"Gimme a D!"

"D!"

"Gimme a Y!"

"Y!"

"What's it spell?" Bella yelled. She ran to the couch and jumped on top of her friend as they all cried, "LADY!"

"Okay, I'll do it," Lady said. "Dad, will you help me?"

"Of course!"

"And I have the perfect group to test your doughnuts," Bella said. "My soccer teammates! They would love to be your testers and write reviews."

Lady shuddered when she imagined a million rough soccer players piling into her clean kitchen. But she knew the team loved to eat! "I love that idea," she said. "Oh Bella, you are the sweetest best friend a doxie could ever have."

The deadline to enter the contest was one week away. In that time, they had to get all the ingredients, make sure they had enough oil and the fryer was ready to go, download and print out the official review forms, and set aside enough time to prep, cook—"And eat!" said Bella.

"Ha, ha," Lady said. "Remember we have to give Mom enough time to take the photos before we start gobbling." Lady's mom was a professional photographer for *Doxie Vogue Magazine*, and she would make sure the doughnuts looked delicious.

Lady had fun going to the store with her dad to buy enough vegetable oil and milk. She had carefully checked in their pantry and refrigerator to be sure they already had eggs, flour, sugar, baking powder, salt, and butter. The night before their big cooking day, Lady set out all her equipment. The star attraction, where all the frying would take place, was the big Dutch oven that sat high on the counter. Lady went to bed almost too tired to sleep. But before she knew it, it was morning and time to start cooking!

Bella burst through the kitchen door right at nine o'clock.

"Hey, Bella!" Lady squeaked with a wiggle. "I'm so nervous! I hope everything turns out okay! What if I don't make it?" Lady's eyes started to tear up a little.

"Don't worry, Lady!" Bella gave her a hug. "You've got this—I believe in you! Let's just pretend we're making doughnuts for a slumber party."

"You're right, Bella. That would be fun no matter what!"

As Lady and Bella scampered around the kitchen, Lady's dad suggested, "Better fill up the soap dispenser because you'll be washing your paws a lot today."

"Yes, Chef Daddy!" Lady yipped.

"Okay!" Bella barked. "But I usually just lick my paws when I need them to be clean."

Lady froze. "Bella, that's gross!"

"Why?" Bella said. "It all goes to the same place."

Lady never understood how Bella could let herself get so dirty all the time. Lady was more dainty. And, she knew the rules of the kitchen. "You better not lick your paws while you're cooking with me!" she said. "This is too important!"

Bella's shoulders sagged. Her feelings were a little hurt.

Lady's dad chimed in, "Take it easy, Chef Lady. Bella doesn't have the kitchen experience you do. Perhaps she doesn't know why it's important to keep her paws clean when cooking."

Lady calmed down and remembered how much fun cooking is, especially when cooking with her best friend. And, she'd really only washed her paws all the time because her dad said so. "Why do we wash all the time, Dad?"

"Washing your paws is the best way to stop germs from spreading. When you're cooking for others, you want to be sure they only get what's good for them, not what's bad."

Bella cheered up. "Is that why my mom is always asking me if I washed my paws before dinner? I certainly don't want to get any yucky germs on the delightfully delicious doughnuts that my teammates are going to eat."

Lady added, "Dad taught me there is a best way to clean paws, too."

"That's right, Chef Lady," Dad answered. "Why don't you share those tips with Bella?"

Lady recited her dad's paw cleaning tips perfectly. "Use warm water, work up a good lather, and wash for twenty seconds. Then rinse and dry with a clean towel every time you wash!"

Bella giggled at the thought of timing how long she washed her paws. "I love

to count! It will be fun to count to twenty every time I wash my paws!"

Lady wiggled and giggled at the thought of Bella counting aloud while she washed her paws. It was fun cooking with her friend!

It was time to get going on making the doughnuts. Lady asked Bella and her dad to join her at the kitchen table as she read her recipe aloud—a good practice before any cooking project.

"Make the glaze first," she began—but Bella interrupted.

"Yay! I love the glaze!" Bella pumped her fist.

Lady giggled and kept reading. The directions soon got too complicated for Bella to follow. "How will we remember all these steps?" she asked.

"We'll keep the recipe nearby, don't worry," Lady's dad said.

Lady read on, about setting up the Dutch oven, about mixing the ingredients, and about heating up the oil. One part was always difficult—dropping the dough into the very hot oil—but Dad was always there to help. Lady wasn't tall enough to stand over the pot at the stove herself, so Dad took care of that step. Young dachshund chefs must be smart and safe when cooking, especially when cooking with hot oil.

When Lady was done reading, Bella jumped up from her seat. "I want to mix ingredients!"

But it turned out that Bella wasn't the best at measuring. She'd fill the cup only halfway and think it was fine, or she'd let the teaspoon mound way over the top. Lady instead showed her how to fill the cups and spoons and then carefully level the ingredient with a dinner knife.

"I never knew it was this exact," Bella exclaimed. "It's like a science project."

"Exactly!" said Lady's dad. "Cooking is like chemistry and physics combined."

Lady giggled and wiggled to think of test tubes and chemicals stewing on her stove. "This tastes a lot better, though."

Bella laughed. "It sure does!"

Soon the yummy glaze was ready. Bella couldn't help licking her fingers before she washed them every time, but Lady tried not to notice. Lady set the glaze aside and gathered and mixed the doughnut ingredients into a large bowl. "I think we're ready for the dough dropping, Dad!"

Both Lady and Bella loved to watch the doughnuts change from sticky dough to perfectly round and brown doughnuts holes as Lady's dad dropped the balls of dough into the hot oil. It was a magical transformation! Both doxie-girls were careful to stay far enough away from the oil so they wouldn't get accidentally spattered. Even Bella knew that was a good idea.

The final task of the fun morning was dipping the slightly cooled doughnuts into the glaze. "This is the best part," Bella barked. "I love dipping the dough-nuts." Lady wiggled and giggled in agreement. They carefully placed each glazed doughnut onto the cooling rack with a cookie sheet under to catch any excess glaze that dripped off.

The clock in the living room chimed eleven. Lady gasped. "Our tasters will be here soon!"

"Wait!" Dad said. "You forgot the most important step."

Lady froze. What could she have forgotten? It was almost too late to do anything else!

But Dad laughed. "A good chef always taste-tests the food before serving it."

Bella wiggled and Lady giggled as they each popped a delightfully delicious doughnut hole into their mouths. "Yummy!" yelled Bella. Lady blushed. They were very good!

Soon the doorbell started buzzing. Lady arranged the dazzling doughnuts onto serving platters while Bella escorted her soccer teammates to the backyard where there were chairs with review cards on them.

Lady's mom was already there, with her camera set up to capture the best images in the sunlight. She photographed the mouthwatering glazed doughnuts on their fancy platters, then got great photos of Bella's teammates as they howled and hooted gleefully and wiggled and giggled with each bite.

Suddenly, Bella shouted out a cheer. "Who's the best at cooking? Who's the best cook ever? Gimme an L!"

The whole soccer team cried, "L!"

"Gimme an A!"

"A!"

Lady wiggled and giggled, so happy that they were all enjoying her cooking as much as she had enjoyed all their games.

Bella kept leading the cheer. "Gimme a D!"

"D!"

"Gimme a Y!"

"Y!"

"What's it spell?" Bella yelled.

The team leaped to their feet and shouted, "LADY!"

Phew! Their doughnut eating party was a resounding success. After the team left and the review cards were gathered, it was time for the one part Lady didn't like very much—cleaning up the kitchen. But Lady knew cleaning after cooking is all part of what it takes to make delightfully delicious doughnuts. Not only is it nice to leave the kitchen tidy and clean for the next person, it also means everything is ready for the next time she wanted to cook. So with lots of wiggles and giggles, Lady and Bella worked hard to get the kitchen cleaned to perfection.

As they cleaned, Lady realized that her recipe had a secret ingredient nobody else's had. She gave her best friend a hug and yelped, "Thank you so much for being here, Bella. The best part of making doughnuts is doing it with you—my very best friend."

Bella hugged her right back. "It was great, Lady! I never knew how hard you work to make all the yummy things you always share. You're the best friend ever!"

When Lady came home from wiener school one day there was a fat envelope addressed to her sitting on the kitchen table. "Bella! Bella!" she yelled across the yard. "It's here!"

Bella came rushing over. From her soccer playing, she knew how great it was to win, but she also knew how disappointing it could be to lose. "No matter what," she said, "remember you're a great chef. We will keep on having fun cooking yummy treats together."

Lady hardly heard her. She ripped open the envelope and read. Then, she started wiggling and giggling all over the kitchen. "I can't believe it! I can't believe it!" Lady squealed and squeaked.

"What?" Bella shouted. "What does it say?"

Lady's dad and mom came running too at all the commotion. Lady flung her arms around everyone, one after the other.

"I get to be on the show!" she shouted.

Everyone cheered. Lady's kitchen had never been so happy.

Lady's dream of meeting Chef Doxter came true. Soon, she was on television as a guest judge while contestants cooked her delightfully delicious doughnuts. And Lady's number one fan, Bella, got a back stage pass to watch her best friend.

Adorable Animal Crackers

Lady says all of your friends will agree that Animal Crackers are absolutely awesome and A-1.

You will need:

- Large mixing bowl
- Large mixing spoon
- Measuring cups
- Measuring spoons
- Microwaveable bowl
- Rolling pin
- Animal cookie cutters
- Cookie sheet
- Spatula
- Potholders
- Waxed paper or cooling rack
- Parchment paper (optional)

Cracker Ingredients:

- 1 cup oatmeal
- ¼ cup honey
- ½ teaspoon salt
- 1½ cups all-purpose flour
- ½ teaspoon baking soda
- ½ cup butter (1 stick)
- ¼ cup buttermilk

Frosting Ingredients:

- 1½ cups vanilla or chocolate chips

"These are healthy cookies, not terribly sweet. They were very fun to make and tasted great when we put melted chocolate on top! Use smaller cookie cutters to get more cookies!"

Photos on page 79 —Paige, age 9, Maryland

Aa

Cracker Directions:

- Preheat oven to 400 degrees.

- Combine oatmeal, salt, flour, and baking soda in the large mixing bowl. Cut in softened butter and honey. Add the buttermilk and stir until combined.

- On a lightly floured surface, roll dough into a ball and flatten a little. Then roll dough very thin (about $\frac{1}{8}$ inch thick) with a rolling pin. Cut with animal cookie cutters that have also been lightly floured.

- Place your amazing "animals" 1 inch apart on a cookie sheet lined with parchment paper.

- Bake for 8 minutes, until edges are lightly browned. Remove hot cookie sheet from oven with potholders. Cool animal crackers on the cookie sheet until they firm up—about 2 minutes. Remove crackers from cookie sheet with a spatula. Finish cooling your animals on waxed paper or a cooling rack.

Frosting Directions:

- Pour vanilla or chocolate chips into a microwaveable bowl and microwave in 30-second increments until just melted. Stir in between each 30 seconds as required. (Chocolate burns easily in the microwave so you'll have to watch it carefully.) Once melted, remove from microwave and continue stirring until smooth.

- With clean hands, dip the cooled animal crackers face down one at a time into the melted chocolate to frost. Frost only the cracker top, or dip entire cracker and frost both top and bottom—your choice!

- Place frosted animal crackers face up on a cooling rack to allow the chocolate to set—at least an hour.

Servings: 24

Best Blueberry Muffins

Bella loves to surprise her best friend with Best Blueberry Muffins because Lady loves blueberries.

You will need:
- Muffin pan
- Measuring cups
- Measuring spoons
- Large mixing bowl
- Small mixing bowl
- Large mixing spoon
- Large dinner spoon
- Muffin cup liners
- Fork
- Potholders
- Cooling rack

Muffin Ingredients:
- 1½ cups all-purpose flour
- ¾ cup sugar
- ½ teaspoon salt
- 2 teaspoons baking powder
- ⅓ cup vegetable oil
- 1 egg
- ½ cup whole milk
- 1 cup fresh blueberries

Crumb Topping Ingredients:
- ½ cup sugar
- ⅓ cup all-purpose flour
- ¼ cup butter
- 1½ teaspoons ground cinnamon

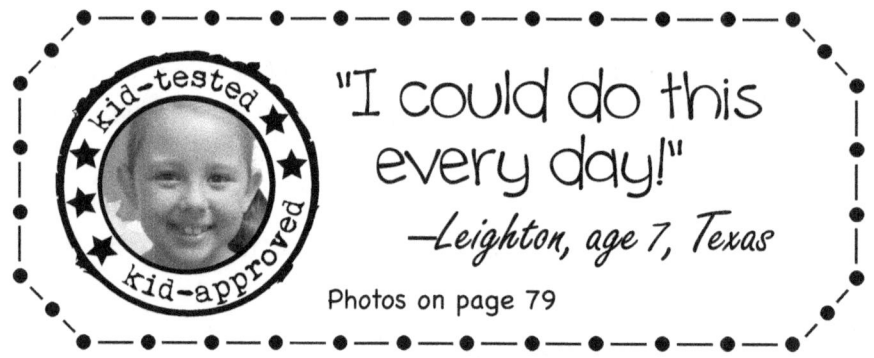

"I could do this every day!"
—Leighton, age 7, Texas

Photos on page 79

Bb

Directions:

- Preheat oven to 400 degrees. Line muffin pan cups with muffin liners.

- Combine muffin dry ingredients in the large mixing bowl: flour, sugar, salt, and baking powder.

- Pour vegetable oil into a 1-cup sized measuring cup. Add the egg and milk to fill the measuring cup, adding more milk if needed to reach the 1-cup mark. Blend this liquid mixture with your flour mixture.

- Stir in blueberries.

- Using a large tablespoon, completely fill muffin cups with your batter.

- Combine the crumb topping ingredients in the small mixing bowl and mix with a fork. Using your clean fingers, sprinkle crumb-topping mixture on top of each filled muffin cup.

- Bake for 25-30 minutes. Using potholders, carefully set muffin pan on cooling rack.

Servings: 12

Cool Cherry Dump Cobbler

Lady is certain your crowd will be completely captivated with your Cool Cherry Dump Cobbler.

You will need:

- 13x9x2 baking pan
- Large spreading spoon
- Microwavable bowl or small saucepan
- Measuring cups
- Potholders

Ingredients:

- 1 can (20 ounce) crushed pineapple w/ juice undrained
- 1 can cherry pie filling
- 1 butter recipe yellow cake mix
- 1 cup finely chopped pecans
- 1 cup melted butter (2 sticks)

"I love all the colors!"
—Chloe, age 8, Ohio

Photos on page 80

Cc

Directions:

- Preheat oven  to 350 degrees.

- Dump pineapple with its juice into pan. Spread evenly.

- Dump in the pie filling and spread over the pineapple.

- Dump in the cake mix, sprinkling the dry cake mix evenly over the cherry layer.

- Dump the pecans over the cake mix.

- Melt butter in a microwavable bowl on HIGH in the microwave for 20-30 seconds or on the stovetop on low heat in a small saucepan and pour on top of the pecan covered cake mix layer.

- Bake for 1 hour, or until top is lightly browned. Serve warm or cool. It's especially yummy when topped with ice cream or whipped cream topping.

Servings: 10-12

Delightfully Delicious Doughnut Holes

Bella is tickled to dazzle her doxie soccer teammates with Delightfully Delicious Doughnuts Holes.

You will need:

Measuring cups
Measuring spoons
Deep-fry thermometer
Large, heavy-bottomed Dutch oven pot
Small cookie scoop with slide bar
Large mixing bowl
2 small mixing bowls
2 mixing spoons
Whisk
Long-handled large metal slotted spoon
2 baking sheets
Cooling rack
Plastic wrap
Paper towels
Microwavable bowl with lid or small saucepan
Tongs
Potholders
2 bottles of vegetable oil for frying

Doughnut Ingredients:

1 cup whole milk
1 large egg
2 cups all-purpose flour
2 tablespoons sugar
4½ teaspoons baking powder
½ teaspoon salt
¼ cup (½ stick) melted butter

Glaze Ingredients:

1½ cups powdered sugar
3-4 tablespoons whole milk
2 teaspoons vanilla extract

Note: Be sure to ask a grown-up to help with the dropping and deep-frying of the doughnuts.

"Delicious! Tip: Be sure to not make them too big or they won't cook all the way through."
—Callista, age 16, Arkansas

Photos on page 80

Glaze Directions:

- Make the glaze first! Add the powdered sugar into a small mixing bowl. Slowly stir in milk, adding one tablespoon at a time, stirring, then adding another. Add the vanilla extract until the mixture is smooth. If the glaze isn't thin enough, add an additional tablespoon of milk. The glaze should be thin enough to pour off of a spoon easily. Cover the mixing bowl with plastic wrap and set it aside while you make the doughnut holes.

Doughnut Directions:

- Pour the vegetable oil into a large, heavy-bottomed Dutch oven pot. You will need at least 2 inches of oil in the pot and at least 2 inches between the top of the oil and the top of the pot. Attach the deep-fry thermometer to the pot, making sure it doesn't touch the bottom of the pan, and begin heating the oil over medium heat to 350 degrees. Line a baking sheet with paper towels and place a cooling rack over the second baking sheet.

- In a small bowl, whisk the milk and the egg until combined well.

- In a large mixing bowl, whisk the flour, sugar, baking powder, and salt. Stir the milk-egg mixture into the dry ingredients. Melt the butter in a microwavable bowl with lid in the microwave for 30 or more seconds or on stovetop in a small saucepan until completely melted. Add the melted butter to the other ingredients, combining until soft dough forms.

- Once the oil has reached 350 degrees, your grown-up helper should use a small cookie scoop with a slide bar to drop about 1 tablespoon scoops of dough into the oil. Be careful not to overcrowd the pan. The dough expands when fried, so a tablespoon of batter will result in a 2-inch doughnut hole. If you prefer smaller doughnuts, drop about 1 teaspoon of batter into the oil. If the amount is too large, the doughnut holes will not cook through. Also, keep a close eye on the thermometer as oil can get too hot quickly. If it does, your grown-up helper can remove pan from heat briefly until the correct temperature is regained.

- Deep-fry the doughnuts, flipping them in the oil for about 2 minutes or until they're golden brown. Using the large metal slotted spoon, lift the doughnuts out of the hot oil to a paper towel-lined baking sheet.

- Allow the doughnuts to cool slightly. Then with tongs or clean fingers one by one roll the doughnuts into the glaze. Set them on the cooling rack with baking sheet under to allow the excess glaze to drip off.

Servings: 6-8 people with 2-3 doughnut holes each

Easy Extraordinary Egg Casserole

Lady is eager and excited to eat her favorite Easy Extraordinary Egg Casserole for breakfast.

You will need:

- 13x9x2 baking pan
- Measuring spoons
- Measuring cups
- Silicone spatula
- Fork
- Large mixing spoon
- Skillet
- Small mixing bowl
- Large mixing bowl
- Potholders
- Cooking spray

Ingredients:

- 6 eggs
- 1 pound pork sausage, browned and drained
- 1 teaspoon dry mustard
- 1 cup all-purpose baking mix (such as Bisquick)
- 1 teaspoon oregano
- 2 cups whole milk
- 1 cup cheddar cheese, shredded

—Cameron, age 10, Texas

"My Easy Extraordinary Egg Casserole was not as easy to make as I thought it would be. It was hard to wait overnight to cook it. The next morning when I cooked it and tasted it, I knew it was worth the wait."

Photos on page 80

Ee

Directions:

🐾 Crack eggs into a small mixing bowl and whisk slightly with a fork.

🐾 Crumble and cook pork sausage in a skillet, stirring with a silicone spatula until completely browned. Drain off any fat.

🐾 In a large mixing bowl, stir dry ingredients together: all-purpose baking mix, dry mustard, and oregano. Add milk, eggs, cheese, and cooked sausage and combine with dry ingredients.

🐾 Spray a 13x9x2 baking pan with cooking spray before pouring your casserole mixture into the pan. Cover and refrigerate overnight.

🐾 The next morning preheat oven to 350 degrees.

🐾 Bake uncovered for 1 hour.

Servings: 12-16

Fluffy Fabulous Flapjacks

Bella says grab your fork and enjoy these fantastic Fluffy Fabulous Flapjacks.

You will need:

- Large non-stick griddle
- Large mixing bowl
- Small mixing bowl
- Small bowl for cracking eggs
- Fork
- Ladle or large spoon
- Mixing spoon
- Measuring spoons
- Measuring cups
- Silicone spatula

Ingredients:

- 2 cups flour
- 1 teaspoon salt
- 3 tablespoons sugar
- 2 tablespoons baking powder
- 2 eggs
- ¼ cup melted butter
- 1¾ cups whole milk
- Butter for topping when done

"Great! Easy to make!"
—Courtney, age 10, Texas

Photos on page 80

28

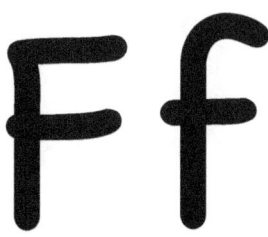

Directions:

🐾 Mix dry ingredients together in the large mixing bowl: flour, salt, sugar, and baking powder.

🐾 Crack eggs one at a time into a small bowl to make sure none are rotten. Then add eggs one at a time into a mixing bowl. Add butter and milk and whisk with a fork.

🐾 Slowly stir the egg, butter, and milk mixture into the large bowl of dry ingredients.

🐾 Mix just until smooth, but do not over mix. Let batter sit at least 10 minutes while heating the griddle.

🐾 With a ladle or large spoon, pour batter onto a hot griddle in small amounts to form small circles.

🐾 Brown flapjacks on both sides, turning with a silicone spatula when small bubbles start to form.

🐾 Place your flapjacks on a plate and top with butter.

Servings: 16 (using ¼ cup batter per serving)

Groovy Graham Crackers

Lady believes Groovy Graham Crackers are perfect for any gala or gift giving.

You will need:

- Measuring cups
- Aluminum foil
- 15x10x1 baking pan
- 1 medium saucepan
- Potholders
- Spatula
- Silicone mixing spoon
- Waxed paper

Ingredients:

- 24 cinnamon graham crackers
- 1 cup light brown sugar
- 1 cup butter (2 sticks)
- 1 cup chopped pecans

kid-tested • kid-approved

"Smells so yummy!"
—Bailey, age 12, Texas

Photos on page 81

30

Directions:

- Preheat oven to 350 degrees. Line your baking pan with aluminum foil, including the sides of the baking pan.

- Lay your graham crackers tightly across the foil-lined baking pan. Trim any crackers to fit the sides of the pan if needed. Set aside.

- In a medium saucepan, bring the butter and sugar to a boil over medium heat, stirring constantly with a silicone (heat resistant) mixing spoon. When mixture begins to bubble, continue cooking for 2 minutes, stirring constantly.

- Remove from heat and stir in pecans. Immediately pour over the graham crackers, spreading evenly and completely covering each cracker.

- Bake for 8 minutes.

- Allow crackers to cool for about 5 minutes before breaking into pieces with spatula and placing on waxed paper to finish cooling completely. Store in an airtight container.

Servings: 14

Horribly Messy Hamburgers

Bella recommends hot Horribly Messy Hamburgers for making your hungry friends happy.

Ingredients:

- 1 pound lean ground beef
- 1½ cups ketchup
- 1 cup chunky salsa
- 2 tablespoons light brown sugar
- 1 tablespoon Worcestershire sauce
- 2 tablespoons white vinegar
- 2 tablespoons Dijon mustard
- 1 teaspoon hot sauce
- 8 small slider buns

You will need:

- Large skillet
- Measuring cups
- Measuring spoons
- Silicone spatula

"The Horribly Messy Hamburgers were filled with juicy taste that my brothers and I devoured. It was pretty sweet with a little kick of hot."
—Ashley, age 9, California

Photos on page 81

Directions:

🐾 Heat a large skillet over medium-high heat and stir in the ground beef. Cook and stir until the beef is crumbly, evenly browned, and no longer pink. Drain and discard any excess grease.

🐾 Stir in ketchup, salsa, brown sugar, Worcestershire sauce, white vinegar, Dijon mustard, and hot sauce. Bring to a simmer and cook, stirring occasionally, over low heat 20-30 minutes.

🐾 Serve on hot slider buns.

Servings: 8

Incredible Ice Cream Nanas

Lady enjoys eating Incredible Ice Cream Nanas inside on hot summer days.

You will need:

- Food processor or blender
- Mixing spoon
- Measuring spoons
- Quart-sized re-sealable baggie
- Knife

Ingredients:

- 6 ripe bananas
- 2 tablespoons creamy peanut butter
- 4 tablespoons honey

"If you like peanut butter and bananas, this is definitely the cool dessert for you!"
—Mack, age 11, California

Photos on page 81

Ii

Directions:

- 🐾 Remove peels and cut bananas into 1-inch pieces, and place in a re-sealable baggie to freeze overnight.

- 🐾 Put the frozen bananas in a food processor or blender and purée, scraping down the sides from time to time until smooth.

- 🐾 Add the peanut butter and honey, and purée another minute or two.

- 🐾 Your ice cream nanas are ready to eat instantly, or you may want to scoop into a freezer bowl and refreeze for an hour.

Servings: 4 small ice cream bowls

Jazzy Popcorn Balls

Bella and her teammates jump for joy when eating Jazzy Popcorn Balls.

You will need:

- Extra-large saucepan or Dutch oven pot
- Waxed paper
- Silicone mixing spoon
- Cooking spray
- Microwave for popping popcorn
- May need extra large mixing bowl

Ingredients:

- ¼ cup (½ stick) butter
- 1 package (10½ ounces) mini-marshmallows
- 1 package (3 ounce) gelatin, your favorite flavor
- 12 cups of popped popcorn (2 bags of microwave popcorn)

"Good!" 👍
—Luke, 4, Texas

Photos on page 81

Jj

Directions:

- 🐾 Buy or pop popcorn.

- 🐾 In a very large saucepan, melt butter and mini-marshmallows on low heat. Stir frequently with a silicone (heat resistant) mixing spoon.

- 🐾 Remove from heat when melted and stir in dry gelatin mix until blended.

- 🐾 Add the popcorn if your large saucepan is large enough, or pour all ingredients into a very large mixing bowl. Toss to coat.

- 🐾 With super clean hands that have been greased well with cooking spray, shape the popcorn into balls and place onto waxed paper for cooling.

Servings: 25

Krazy Dog Kebobs

Lady says it's kooky fun to make Krazy Dog Kebobs.

You will need:

- Microwaveable dish or oven broiler pan or outdoor grill
- Measuring spoons
- Knife
- Toothpicks, metal, or wood skewers
- Grill tongs
- Gallon-size re-sealable baggie
- Small mixing bowl
- Mixing spoon
- Potholders

Ingredients:

- 1 (13-ounce) can chunk pineapple—drain and save juice
- 2 tablespoons soy sauce
- 3 tablespoons dark brown sugar
- 1 tablespoon apple cider vinegar
- 6 hot dogs—cut into 36 pieces (6 pieces per hotdog)

Note: Grown-up helper will be needed if outdoor grilling.

Photos on page 82

"These were so yummy! I'm making some to take with me camping to share with my buddies!"

—Sadler, age 9, Texas

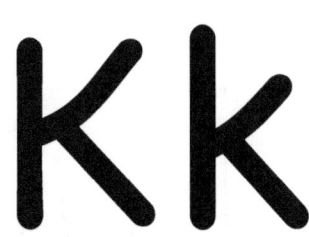

Directions:

 Make a marinade by combining the juice you saved from your chunk pineapple can with soy sauce, brown sugar, and vinegar in a small mixing bowl.

 Place your cut hot dogs and pineapple chunks into a re-sealable baggie and pour in the marinade. Seal and place baggie in refrigerator for 30 minutes to 1 hour before cooking.

 Arrange hot dog pieces and pineapple chunks on toothpicks if cooking in a microwave or metal or wood skewers if you're going to cook on an outdoor grill or on a broiler pan in the oven. If using wood skewers, be sure to soak skewers in cold water for at least an hour prior to cooking.

 For cooking in a microwave, place your marinated kebobs on toothpicks into a microwaveable dish. Microwave on high for 45 seconds. Turn with tongs. Cook an additional 45 seconds.

 If using outdoor grill, place kebobs on skewers on rack over medium heat for 1-2 minutes each side. Using grill tongs, turn at least twice if not 3 times.

 If using a broiler pan in oven, place kebobs on skewers in oven at 350 degrees for 20 minutes. Broil on low heat for final 30 seconds to a minute to brown them, watching closely so they don't get too brown. Carefully remove hot pan from oven with potholders.

Servings: 6 if on long skewers, or 36 appetizers

Lucky Cheese Log

Bella loves eating Lucky Cheese Log with her favorite wafers or apple slices.

You will need:

- Large mixing bowl
- Mixing spoon
- Measuring cups
- Measuring spoons
- Plastic wrap
- Waxed paper
- 13x9x2 baking pan

Ingredients:

- 8 ounces whipped cream cheese tub
- 2 tablespoons softened butter
- ¼ cup creamy peanut butter
- ¼ cup powdered sugar
- 2 tablespoons light brown sugar
- 3 tablespoons cocoa powder
- ½ tablespoon vanilla extract
- ¾ cup mini-chocolate chips

"Awesome! I love peanut butter and chocolate!"
—Cooper, age 6, Texas

Photos on page 82

Ll

Directions:

- In a large mixing bowl, cream together the cream cheese, softened butter, and peanut butter.

- Add the powdered sugar, brown sugar, cocoa powder, and vanilla extract. Mix well.

- Cover bowl with plastic wrap and chill in refrigerator overnight.

- The next day, put mixture on waxed paper. Use the waxed paper to help you roll your cheese mixture into a log.

- Place mini-chocolate chips in a 13x9x2 baking pan. Roll and coat the chilled cheese log in mini-chocolate chips until covered. Dust lightly with powdered sugar.

Servings: 8-10

Merry Marshmallow Brownies

Lady says Merry Marshmallow Brownies are marvelous and magnificent for any occasion.

You will need:

- Small saucepan
- Silicone mixing spoon
- Large mixing bowl
- Small mixing bowl
- Measuring cups
- Measuring spoons
- Potholders
- Electric mixer
- Toothpick
- Cooling rack
- 13x9x2 baking pan

Ingredients:

- 1 cup butterscotch chips
- ½ cup butter, cubed
- 2 eggs
- ⅔ cup light brown sugar
- 1 teaspoon vanilla extract
- 1½ cups all-purpose flour
- 2 teaspoons baking powder
- ½ teaspoon salt
- 2 cups miniature marshmallows
- 2 cups (12 ounces) semi-sweet chocolate chips
- ½ cup chopped walnuts (optional)

"They are so sweet and yummy!"
—Leila, age 4, Germany

Photos on page 82

42

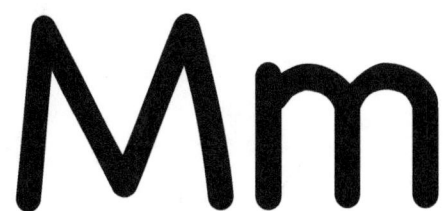

Directions:

- Preheat oven  to 325 degrees.

- In a small saucepan,  melt butterscotch chips and butter, stirring constantly with silicone (heat resistant) mixing spoon until smooth. Remove from heat and cool for 10 minutes.

- In a large mixing bowl with electric mixer, beat the eggs, brown sugar, and vanilla until blended. Beat in butterscotch mixture.

- Combine the flour, baking powder, and salt in a small mixing bowl. Gradually add to the batter and beat until mixed well. Stir in the marshmallows, chocolate chips and nuts.

- Spread into a greased 13x9x2 baking pan and bake for 35-40 minutes or until a toothpick inserted near the center comes out clean. Do not over bake! Cool completely on a wire rack.

Servings: 15

Nifty Nutty Snowballs

Bella says Nifty Nutty Snowballs are neat to eat and nice to share.

You will need:

- 2 medium mixing bowls
- Large mixing spoon
- Spatula
- Cookie sheet
- Parchment paper (optional)
- Measuring cups
- Measuring spoons
- Cooling rack

Ingredients:

- 3 cups all-purpose flour
- ½ cup crushed pecans
- ¾ cup powdered sugar
- 1 tablespoon vanilla extract
- 1½ cup butter (3 sticks softened at room temperature)
- ½ teaspoon salt
- Coating: 1 cup powdered sugar

"These cookies were perfectly crunchy (but not hard) and not too sweet. They were delicious! Make sure not to roll in too much confectioner's sugar—it will all come off and makes a mess. I learned that powdered sugar and confectioner's sugar are the same kind of sugar."

—Chloe, age 12, Maryland

Photos on page 82

Directions:

- 🐾 Preheat the oven to 375 degrees and if using a regular cookie sheet, line with parchment paper.

- 🐾 In one of the mixing bowls, mix dry ingredients together—flour, nuts, salt.

- 🐾 In the other mixing bowl, cream the 3 sticks of softened butter with ¾ cup powdered sugar and the vanilla. Combine with the dry ingredients.

- 🐾 With your clean hands, form the dough into small balls no larger than a whole pecan and place on the cookie sheet, spaced at least an inch apart from each other.

- 🐾 Bake for 10 minutes or until just turning brown. Do not allow these cookies to get too brown. It's better to undercook them than to overcook them. Remove cookie sheet from oven with potholders and let cookies stand on cookie sheet for about 2 minutes.

- 🐾 While they are still warm but cool enough to touch, roll the cookies in powdered sugar. Set coated cookies on cooling rack to cool completely.

Servings: 56

Outstanding Orange Drink

Lady says anyone who has a glass of Outstanding Orange Drink will be overjoyed.

Ingredients:
- 1 (6 ounce) can frozen orange juice
- 1 cup whole milk
- 1 cup water
- ½ cup sugar
- 1 teaspoon vanilla extract
- 12 cubes of ice

You will need:
- Blender
- Measuring cups
- Measuring spoons

"My Outstanding Orange Drink was good. My taste buds loved it!"

—Lindsey, age 7, Texas

Photos on page 83

Directions:

🐾 In a blender, 🍶 blend the frozen orange juice, milk, water, sugar, and vanilla.

🐾 Add ice cubes 🧊 and blend until smooth.

Servings: 4 8-ounce glasses

Pepperoni Pizza Puffs

Bella prefers to serve Pepperoni Pizza Puffs on pink paper plates.

You will need:

- Measuring cups
- Measuring spoons
- Large mixing bowl
- Large mixing fork
- 2 24-cup mini-muffin pans
- Cooking spray

Ingredients:

- 2 cups all-purpose flour
- 2 teaspoons baking powder
- 2 tablespoons Italian seasoning
- 1 cup shredded Parmesan cheese
- 1 teaspoon sugar
- 2 tablespoons extra virgin olive oil
- 1½ cups whole milk
- 2 eggs, beaten
- 2 cups shredded 4-cheese pizza blend
- 1 5-ounce package mini pepperoni rounds
- Favorite marinara sauce for garnish

"So yummy! My new favorite lunchtime snack."
—Khloe, age 4, Oregon

Photos on page 83

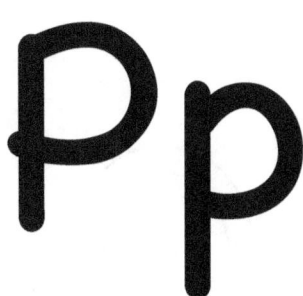

Directions:

- Preheat oven to 350 degrees. Grease your mini-muffin pans with cooking spray.

- In a large bowl, combine flour, baking powder, Italian seasoning, Parmesan cheese, olive oil, sugar, milk, and egg. Stir together with a large mixing fork. Stir in the pizza blend cheese and pepperoni. Mix batter until well blended.

- Add one heaping tablespoon scoop to each muffin cup.

- Bake until golden brown, about 20 minutes.

- Cool for 5 minutes before removing muffin tin.

- Serve with your favorite marinara sauce.

Servings: 50 mini muffins

Quick Quiche Cups

Lady says you'll feel like kings and queens when you eat Quick Quiche Cups.

You will need:

- Muffin pan
- Measuring cups
- Measuring spoons
- Large mixing bowl
- Large mixing spoon
- Rolling pin
- Small spatula
- Potholders
- Cooking Spray

Ingredients:

- 1 3-ounce package cream cheese, softened to room temperature
- ⅔ cup sour cream
- 2 eggs
- ½ cup shredded Swiss cheese
- 4 bacon strips cooked and crumbled, or 4 tablespoons if using already cooked and crumbled bacon
- 2 tablespoons finely chopped sweet red pepper
- ¼ teaspoon dried oregano
- 1 10-ounce tube refrigerated biscuits (tube of 5 biscuits)
- Flour for dusting muffin pan cups

kid-tested kid-approved

"The baking was a lot of fun, and the quiches were yummy. I also passed them out to my family and everyone thought they were yummy, too."

—Berghan, age 8, Florida

Photos on page 83

Directions:

- 🐾 Preheat oven to 375 degrees. Spray muffin pan with cooking spray and lightly dust with flour in each muffin pan cup.

- 🐾 In a large mixing bowl, mix cream cheese and sour cream until smooth. Add the eggs and mix well.

- 🐾 Stir in Swiss cheese, crumbled bacon, bell pepper, and oregano. Set aside.

- 🐾 Cut the 5 biscuit dough rounds in half, making 10 dough rounds. Roll each round flat using your rolling pin, making 10 5-inch circles. Press onto the bottom and sides of the 10 greased muffin cups.

- 🐾 Divide the egg mixture among the biscuit-lined muffin cups, using about 2 tablespoons for each.

- 🐾 Bake for 15-20 minutes or until a toothpick inserted near the center comes out clean.

- 🐾 Remove the muffin pan from oven using potholders. Let it stand for 5 minutes before serving, carefully removing the Quick Quiche Cups with a small spatula.

Servings: 10

Rich Crispy Rice Treats

Bella says eating Rich Crispy Rice Treats will rock your world.

You will need:

Large saucepan
Measuring cups
Measuring spoons
13x9x2 dish
Silicone mixing spoon
Small saucepan
Cooking spray

Ingredients:

7 tablespoons butter, divided into 4 and 3 tablespoons
7 cups miniature marshmallows
½ cup peanut butter
7 cups plain crispy rice breakfast cereal (such as Rice Krispies)
24 peanut butter cups, unwrapped
1½ cups chocolate chips

"They taste impeccable!"
—Avery, age 12, Florida

Photos on page 83

Rr

Directions:

🐾 Melt 4 tablespoons butter over low heat in a large saucepan. Add the marshmallows and stir until completely melted. Stir in the peanut butter.

🐾 Pour the cereal into the marshmallow mixture and stir until completely combined. Press about ⅓ of the cereal mixture into a buttered 13x9x2 pan.

🐾 Place the 24 peanut butter cups over the top of the crispy rice mixture in the pan. Spoon the rest of the crispy rice mixture over the top and press down with super clean hands that have been greased with cooking spray or butter. Let cool completely.

🐾 Place the chocolate chips and remaining 3 tablespoons of butter in a small saucepan and heat on a low heat until melted. Stir until creamy. Spread over the top of the Rich Crispy Rice Treats.

🐾 Cool completely before cutting into squares. Store in a sealed container.

Servings: 24

Spaghetti in a Skillet

Lady gets super big smiles when she serves this savory, sweet spaghetti.

You will need:

- Large deep Dutch oven pot
- Measuring cup
- Measuring spoons
- Large silicone spoon

Ingredients:

- 1 pound very lean ground beef
- 1 finely chopped onion
- 1 tablespoon chili powder
- 1½ teaspoons oregano
- 1 tablespoon sugar
- 1 teaspoon garlic salt
- 1 6-ounce can basil-garlic-oregano tomato paste
- 1 8-ounce can basil-garlic-oregano tomato sauce
- 1 large jar chunky picante sauce
- 1 cup water (may need more)
- 15 ounces of your favorite pasta
- Grated Parmesan cheese for garnish

Photos on page 84

Isaac gave it a thumbs up!

"This is amazing. We just put in a pot and stir it. It's easy."
—Charles

Dylan said in sign language, "E-A-T."

"It has flavor and everything. This is the best I ever had. I'm going to make it at home. It was easy putting everything in the pot."
—Austin

"I love it. I like stirring everything together. I like everything, but the onion made me cry."
—Shelby

—Mr. Greenwood's Gang, Mineral Wells Jr. High, Texas

54

Ss

Directions:

- 🐾 In a large deep Dutch oven pot, brown ground beef on medium-high heat. Cook and stir with silicone (heat resistant) spoon until the beef is crumbly, evenly browned, and no longer pink. Drain and discard any excess grease.

- 🐾 Put cooked, drained beef back into the Dutch oven pot and stir in chopped onion, chili powder, oregano, sugar, and garlic salt.

- 🐾 Blend in tomato paste. Stir in tomato sauce, picante sauce, and water. Bring to a bubbly boil.

- 🐾 Carefully add uncooked pasta and stir to mix in. Cover; reduce heat to a low simmer, stirring slowly and frequently, for 30 minutes.

- 🐾 Serve with grated Parmesan cheese.

Note: Sometimes you may need to add more water depending on how thick or thin you like your spaghetti sauce.

Servings: 6

Tasty French Toast

Bella likes a tall glass of tangy juice with her Tasty French Toast.

You will need:

- 13x9x2 baking pan
- Measuring cups
- Measuring spoons
- Large mixing bowl
- Whisk
- Large mixing spoon
- Medium mixing bowl
- Fork
- Quart-size re-sealable baggie

Toast Ingredients:

- Thickly sliced sweet bread
- 8 eggs
- 2 cups whole milk
- ½ cup heavy whipping cream
- ½ cup sugar
- ½ cup brown sugar
- 2 tablespoons vanilla extract
- Butter, for greasing pan

Topping Ingredients:

- ½ cup all-purpose flour
- ½ cup light brown sugar
- 1 teaspoon ground cinnamon
- ¼ teaspoon salt
- 1 teaspoon ground nutmeg
- 1 stick butter, softened to room temperature, cut into pieces

"This recipe was fun because I got to crack the eggs and mix with my hands."

—Addi, age 5, Texas

Photos on page 84

Tt

Topping Directions:

- Mix the flour, brown sugar, cinnamon, salt, and nutmeg in a medium mixing bowl. Stir together using a fork. Add the butter pieces. Combine with clean hands until the mixture resembles fine pebbles. Store in a baggie in the refrigerator overnight.

Toast Directions:

- Grease the baking pan with butter. Slice bread and evenly distribute slices to cover the bottom of the pan.

- Crack the eggs in a large mixing bowl. Whisk together the eggs, milk and cream. Stir in the sugar, brown sugar, and vanilla. Pour evenly over the bread.

- Cover the pan tightly and store in the refrigerator overnight.

- When you're ready to bake your Tasty French Toast, preheat oven to 350 degrees.

- Remove toast pan from the refrigerator and sprinkle the topping over the top.

- Bake for 45 minutes for a softer, more bread pudding texture, or bake for 1 hour for a firmer, crisper texture.

- Garnish options for putting on top of the French toast: powdered sugar, maple syrup, coconut syrup, jelly, or fruit.

Servings: 4-6

Upside Down Cupcakes

Lady says these unique Upside Down Cupcakes are unusually good.

You will need:

- Small mixing bowl
- Large mixing bowl
- Measuring cup
- Measuring spoons
- 12-cup muffin pan
- Cookie sheet
- Cooling rack
- Potholders
- 2 large mixing spoons
- Small microwaveable bowl or small saucepan
- Small spoon

Ingredients:

- 3 tablespoons melted butter
- 1 16-ounce can of pineapple slices (drain and save 1 cup pineapple juice)
- $\frac{2}{3}$ cup light brown sugar
- 1 cup white sugar
- $\frac{1}{3}$ cup shortening
- 1 egg
- 1 teaspoon vanilla
- $1\frac{1}{4}$ cups all-purpose flour
- 1 teaspoon salt
- 1 teaspoon baking powder

"Delicious!"
—Mason, age 4, Pennsylvania

Photos on page 84

Uu

Directions:

- Preheat oven to 350 degrees.

- Melt butter in a small microwaveable bowl in the microwave for 20-30 seconds or melt in a small saucepan on stovetop. Evenly divide melted butter with a small spoon into the muffin pan cups.

- Drain pineapple slices can, saving 1 cup of the drained juice. Put 1 pineapple slice in each muffin pan cup.

- Evenly divide the brown sugar on top of each pineapple slice, using your clean fingers to crumble the brown sugar.

- In a large mixing bowl, cream sugar and shortening. Crack and add egg and vanilla. Beat together, mixing well.

- In a small mixing bowl, mix the flour, salt, and baking powder. Add these dry ingredients to the large mixing bowl mixture. Stir well, while adding the pineapple juice.

- Evenly divide this mixture on top of the pineapple slices and brown sugar in the muffin pan cups.

- Bake for 30-40 minutes. With potholders, remove from oven and set hot muffin pan on cooling rack for about 10 minutes, till the pan is cool enough to touch.

- Flip muffin pan upside down onto a cookie sheet.

Servings: 12

Velvety Mac and Cheese

Bella recommends Velvety Mac and Cheese as a victorious crowd pleaser.

Mac and Cheese Ingredients:

- 8-ounce package of your favorite pasta, uncooked
- 2 tablespoons butter for greasing baking dish and tossing cooked pasta
- 2½ tablespoons butter, melted
- 2 tablespoons all-purpose flour
- ½ teaspoon salt
- ¼ teaspoon pepper
- 1¾ cups whole milk
- 8 ounces creamy cheese, cubed (such as Velveeta)

You will need:

- Large saucepan
- Large silicone spoon
- Whisk
- Measuring cups
- Measuring spoons
- 1-quart baking dish
- Small microwavable bowl or small saucepan
- Small mixing spoon
- Potholders
- Colander

Topping Ingredients:

- ⅓ cup seasoned bread crumbs
- 1 tablespoon butter

"This dish was very fun to make and tasted so delicious!"
—Audrey, age 8, Massachusetts
Photos on page 84

- 🐾 Preheat oven to 375 degrees. Grease baking dish with 1 tablespoon butter.

- 🐾 Cook pasta in a large saucepan according to the directions on the package and drain well in a colander. Add 1 tablespoon of butter and toss pasta to coat with butter.

- 🐾 In a large saucepan, melt 2½ tablespoons butter over medium heat. With a silicone spoon, stir in flour, salt, and pepper until smooth. Gradually add milk. Stirring with a whisk can help in smoothing the cream sauce. Add cubes of cheese and stir with silicone (heat resistant) spoon until cheese is melted. Stir in cooked pasta until well coated with cheese sauce.

- 🐾 Pour cheese-sauce-coated pasta into a buttered baking dish.

- 🐾 Melt 1 tablespoon butter in a small microwavable bowl for 20 seconds or melt over low heat in a small saucepan on stovetop. Stir the breadcrumbs into the melted butter. Sprinkle crumb mixture on top over the mac and cheese in the baking dish.

- 🐾 Bake, uncovered, for 25–30 minutes or until heated through and topping is golden brown.

Servings: 4-6

Wacky Wheat Wafers

Lady says these warm Wacky Wheat Wafers are wonderful topped with butter, peanut butter, honey, or jelly.

You will need:
- Large skillet
- Large mixing bowl
- Large mixing spoon
- Waxed paper
- Measuring cups
- Measuring spoons
- Cookie sheet
- Paper towels

Ingredients:
- 1 cup all-purpose flour
- 1 cup whole-wheat flour
- 4 teaspoons baking powder
- 1 teaspoon salt
- ⅓ cup vegetable oil
- ¾ cup whole milk
- 4 tablespoons (½ stick) butter

"They taste great! But they were even better with jelly!!"
—Nathan, age 10, Oklahoma

Photos on page 85

Directions:

- 🐾 In a large mixing bowl, combine all-purpose and wheat flours, baking powder, and salt.

- 🐾 Stir in vegetable oil and milk.

- 🐾 Divide dough into 20 parts onto a sheet of waxed paper. Knead each dough section for about a minute and roll into balls. Press the dough balls flat to about $\frac{1}{8}$-inch thick (as thin as you can get them).

- 🐾 Melt butter in a large skillet over medium heat.

- 🐾 Place dough patties into the skillet and fry on each side, flipping with silicone spatula, for about 4 minutes each side, or until brown.

- 🐾 Lift out wafers with silicone spatula onto a cookie sheet lined with paper towels. Serve warm or after cooling.

Servings: **24**

Xcellent Snack Mix

Bella loves to fix this extra yummy snack mix when relaxing and watching television.

You will need:

- Extra large mixing bowl
- Large mixing spoon
- Measuring cups
- Measuring spoons
- 1-quart microwaveable bowl or small saucepan
- Small mixing spoon
- 2-gallon re-sealable baggie
- Waxed paper
- Airtight storage container to hold 9 cups of snack mix

Ingredients:

- 9 cups using a medley of your favorite crunchy cereals (such as Chex, Cheerios, Mini-Shredded Wheat, and others)
- 1 cup semisweet chocolate chips
- ½ cup creamy peanut butter
- ¼ cup butter
- 1 teaspoon vanilla extract
- 1 cup powdered sugar

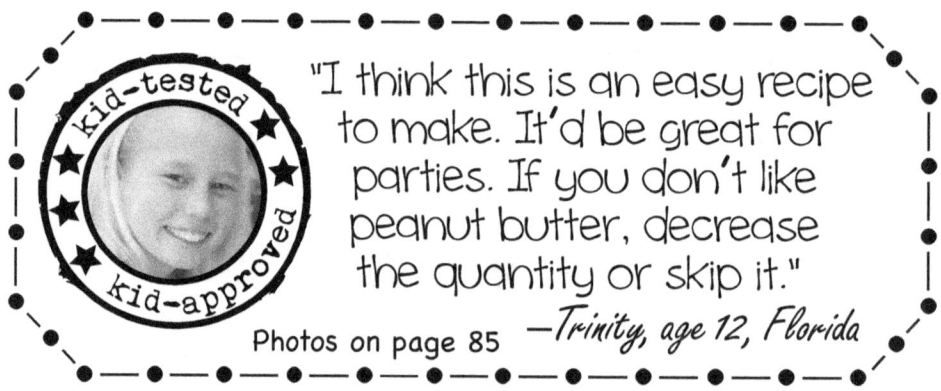

"I think this is an easy recipe to make. It'd be great for parties. If you don't like peanut butter, decrease the quantity or skip it."
—Trinity, age 12, Florida

Photos on page 85

Directions:

- 🐾 Measure cereal and pour into an extra large mixing bowl.

- 🐾 In 1-quart microwaveable bowl, microwave chocolate chips, peanut butter, and butter uncovered on high for 1 minute. Stir. Microwave 30 seconds longer or until mixture can be stirred smooth. Or melt chocolate chips, peanut butter, and butter in a small saucepan on stovetop, stirring constantly until well mixed and melted.

- 🐾 Stir in vanilla extract.

- 🐾 Pour mixture over cereal. Gently stir until evenly coated.

- 🐾 Pour coated Chex into a 2-gallon baggie. Add powdered sugar. Seal bag and toss until well coated.

- 🐾 Spread Xcellent Snack Mix out on waxed paper to cool. Store in airtight container in refrigerator.

Servings: 8-10 small snack servings

Yummy Yogurt Smoothie

Lady has a Yummy Yogurt Smoothie in the morning or for an afternoon snack.

You will need:

- Blender
- Measuring cups
- Measuring spoons
- Knife
- Quart-size re-sealable baggie (optional)

Ingredients:

- 2 cups of ice
- 3 large bananas cut into 1-inch chunks
- 1 cup whole milk
- 1 6-ounce vanilla yogurt
- 3 tablespoons chocolate hazelnut spread (such as Nutella)

"Really easy and really good!"
—Weston, age 7, Texas

Photos on page 85

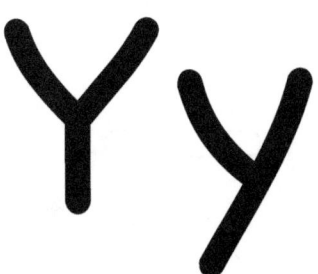

Directions:

🐾 Place ice in the bottom of a blender. Two cups of ice will make your smoothie thick like a milkshake. If you want it more like a juice drink, use less ice—maybe 1 or 2 handfuls.

🐾 If you plan your smoothie the night before, you can peel and slice your bananas into 1-inch chunks, putting the slices into a baggie and freeze overnight. Then you might need less ice. But you can use unfrozen bananas with however much ice that you want for your desired consistency.

🐾 Add the remaining ingredients. Purée until smooth.

Servings: 4-6

Zesty Zucchini Chips

Bella gets zippy when she dips Zesty Zucchini Chips in her favorite salsa.

You will need:

- Measuring cups
- Measuring spoons
- Medium mixing bowl
- Whisk
- Small shallow bowl
- Ovenproof wire rack
- Cookie sheet
- Cooking spray

Ingredients:

- ½ cup plain breadcrumbs
- ½ cup grated fresh Parmesan cheese
- ¼ teaspoon seasoned salt (such as Nature's Seasoning)
- ¼ teaspoon garlic powder
- ⅛ teaspoon freshly ground black pepper
- ¼ cup milk
- 2½ cups ¼-inch thick zucchini slices

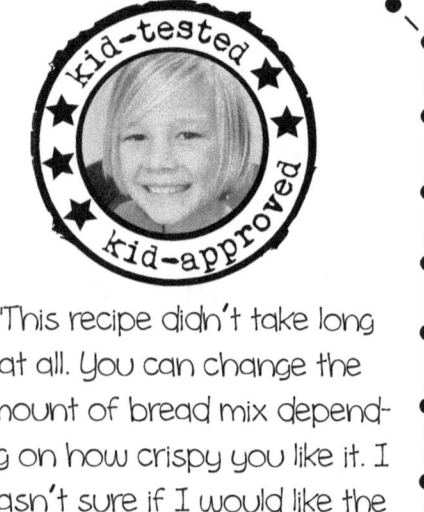

"This recipe didn't take long at all. You can change the amount of bread mix depending on how crispy you like it. I wasn't sure if I would like the chips, but I really did!"

—Holland, age 9, Florida

Photos on page 85

Zz

Directions:

- 🐾 Preheat oven to 425 degrees.

- 🐾 Combine breadcrumbs, Parmesan cheese, seasoned salt, garlic powder, and pepper in a mixing bowl, stirring with a whisk.

- 🐾 Place milk in a shallow bowl.

- 🐾 Dip zucchini slices in milk, and dredge slices in breadcrumb mixture.

- 🐾 Place coated zucchini slices on an ovenproof wire rack coated with cooking spray. Place rack on a cookie sheet.

- 🐾 Bake for 25-30 minutes or until browned and crisp.

Option: If you want a thicker coating on your chips, you can mix an egg with your milk and dip your zucchini slices in this milk/egg mixture before dredging in your breadcrumb mixture.

Servings: 4

Cooking Terms Glossary

Bake: To cook in the oven.

Baste: To brush liquids such as fat, meat drippings, marinade, water, or juices over meat during roasting to add flavor and to prevent the meat from drying out.

Batter: A mixture of flour, butter, shortening or oil, and liquid. Batter is usually for cakes, cookies, or muffins. Batter is more liquid than dough; unlike dough, it cannot be formed into a ball or keep its shape.

Beat: To beat means to stir or mix ingredients with a whisk, spoon, or a mixer.

Blend: To add ingredients together and blend them with a whisk, spoon, or a mixer.

Boil: To cook a liquid such as water or broth so it reaches a boiling temperature. You will see bubbles on the surface and in the pan.

Bread: To coat an ingredient with breadcrumbs, cracker crumbs, or other crumb mixture before cooking it.

Brown: To sauté meat or vegetables or cook flapjacks in a frying pan with oil or butter until they turn brown in color.

Brush: To use a pastry brush to coat the top of the food with melted butter or egg white.

Chill: To place in refrigerator.

Chop: To cut food into pieces with a knife, food chopper, blender, or food processor.

Cooking Terms Glossary

Coat: To cover both sides of a food with flour, powdered sugar, crumbs, chocolate chips, or batter. (See bread.)

Combine: To add ingredients together and stir until evenly distributed.

Cream: To mix butter, shortening, or margarine with sugar or to mix cream cheese with other ingredients until smooth and creamy.

Cube: To cut foods such as vegetables or meat into pieces with equal sides.

Cut in: To blend or cream butter or shortening into a flour mixture with a knife or spatula.

Dash: Less than 1/16 teaspoon. (Since there is no 1/16 teaspoon, use the amount you can pinch between your fingers.)

Deep Fry: To cook food completely covered in hot oil.

Dice: To cut food into small cubes.

Dough: A combination of flour, liquid, and other ingredients that makes a firm mixture that can be shaped for bread, cookies, or doughnuts.

Dredge: To lightly coat food with flour, breadcrumbs, or cracker crumbs. (See coat.)

Drizzle: To pour a liquid over food in a slow, light trickle.

Dust: To sprinkle food with flour, spices, or sugar. (For example, before kneading dough, dust the counter top with flour.)

Cooking Terms Glossary

Dutch oven pot: Any large, heavy pot with a tightly fitting lid, suitable for stovetop or oven use

Fry: To cook food in hot oil or butter until browned or cooked through.

Garnish: To add an edible decoration to make food more attractive or add extra flavors.

Glaze: To coat food with a mixture that gives a shiny appearance. (For example, a chocolate or vanilla glaze on a doughnut.)

Grease: To coat or rub a pan with oil, shortening, butter, or a cooking spray. (For cakes, you grease and dust the pan with flour.)

Grill: To cook food over direct heat on a grill or direct flame.

Ice: To spread a glaze or frosting on a cake or cookie.

Knead: To massage dough with clean hands in a back and forth pressing and folding motion for several minutes until dough is smooth.

Marinate: To season food by placing it in a flavorful mixture prior to cooking, sometimes using a zip-closure baggie and chilling in the refrigerator.

Microwave: To cook, melt, soften, or warm food in a microwave oven.

Mix: To stir ingredients together with a spoon or a mixer until well combined.

Pan fry: To cook with a small amount of oil or butter.

Parchment: Heat-resistant paper used in baking.

Cooking Terms Glossary

Peel: To remove the outer skin of fruit and vegetables with a knife or vegetable peeler.

Pinch: To add less than 1/16 teaspoon. (See dash.)

Purée: To blend food together until it becomes completely smooth.

Sauté: To cook food in hot oil in a pan.

Season: To flavor meat with salt, pepper or other spices.

Sift: To remove lumps from dry ingredients with a mesh strainer or flour sifter.

Simmer: To cook over low heat so food or liquid doesn't reach the boiling point.

Skewer: A wood or metal stick used for cooking on a stick.

Stir: To blend ingredients together.

Stir Fry: To fry cut meat and vegetables on medium-high heat with a small amount of oil or butter.

Strain: To use a colander or strainer to drain liquid off of cooked food.

Thin: To add more liquid to food.

Toss: To mix ingredients with a tossing motion gently to combine.

Whip: To beat ingredients together quickly with a spoon, fork, or mixer until light and fluffy.

Whisk: To mix together by beating with a whisk, fork, or mixer.

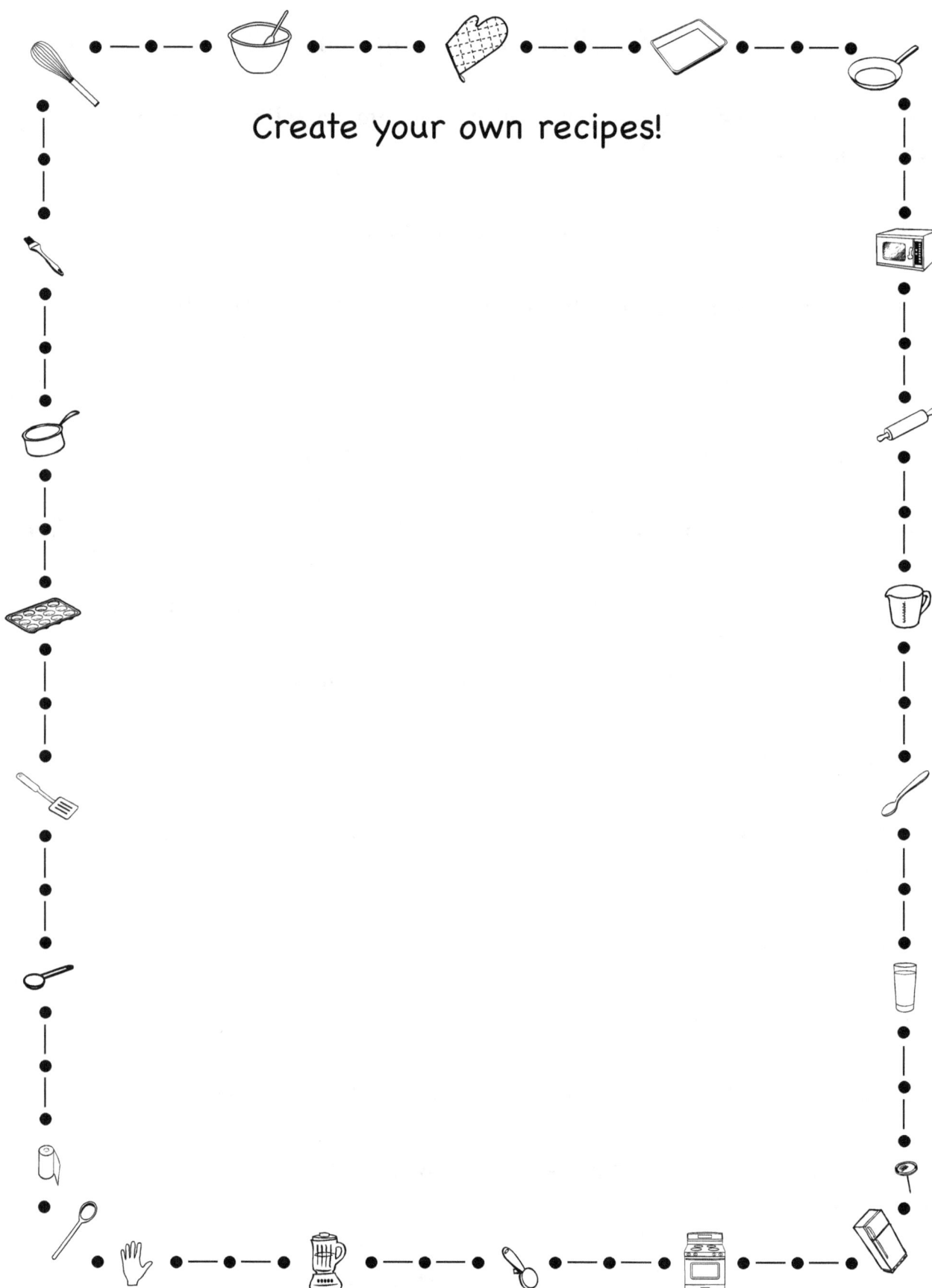

Create your own recipes!

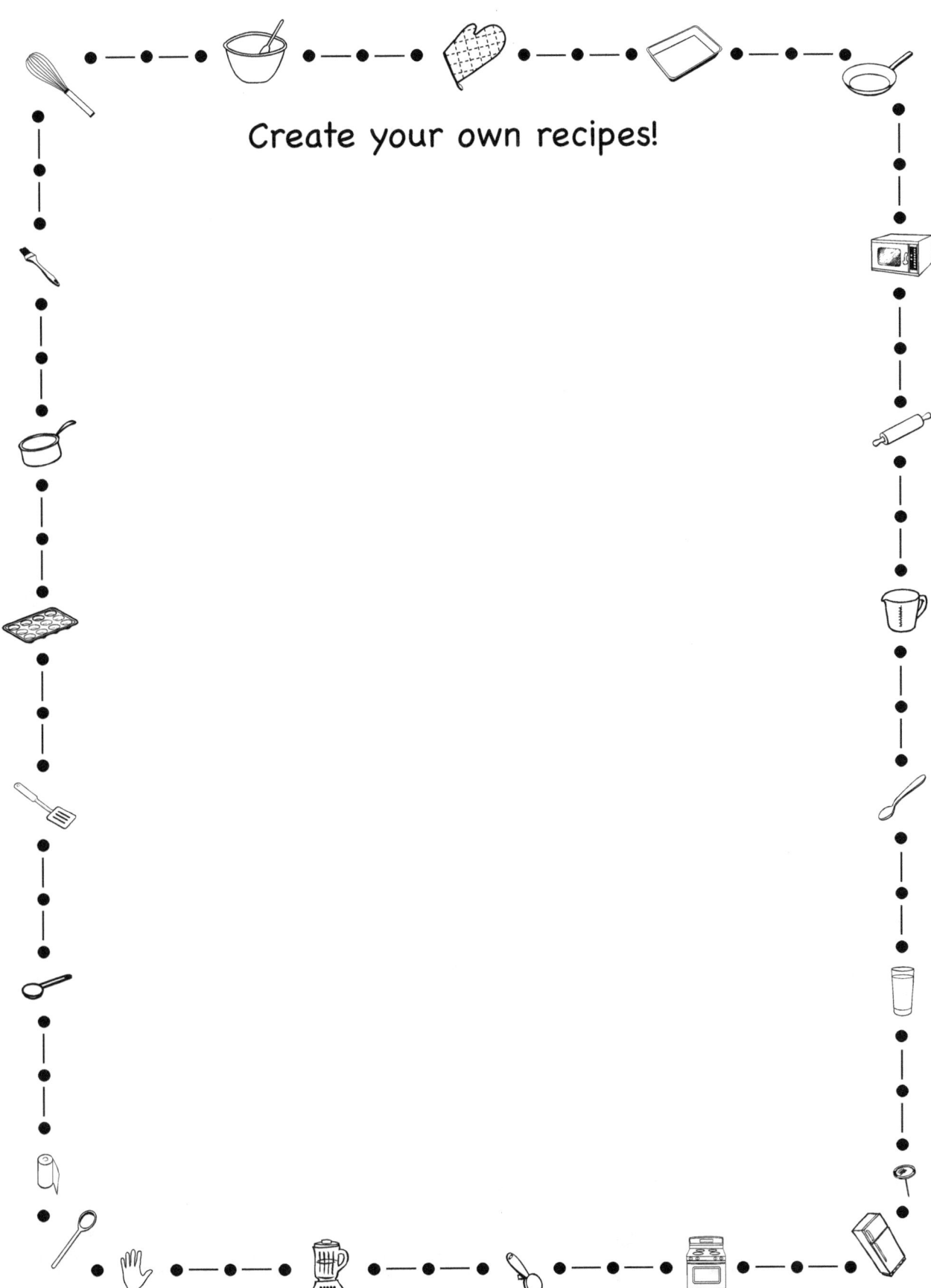

Create your own recipes!

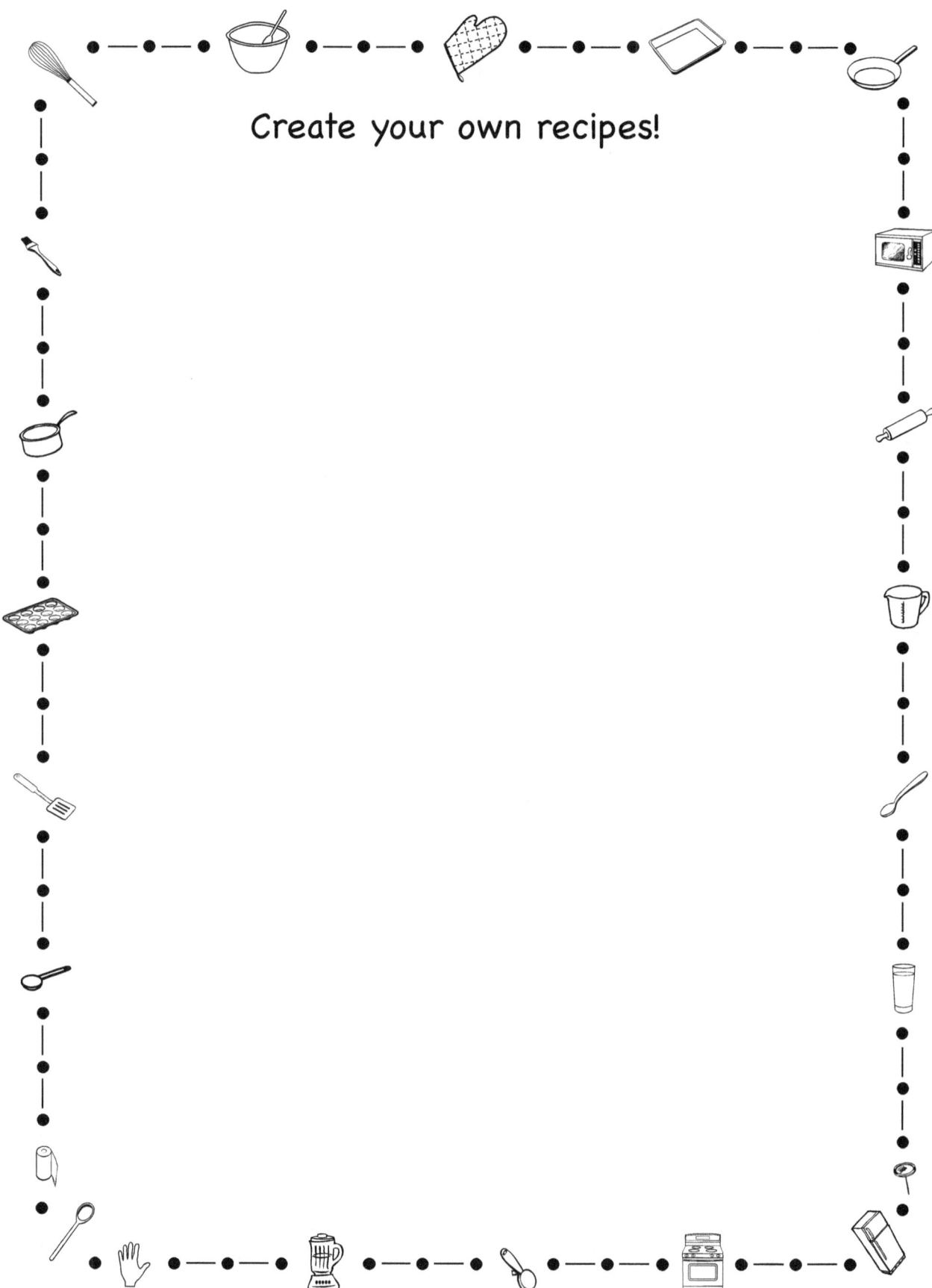

Create your own recipes!

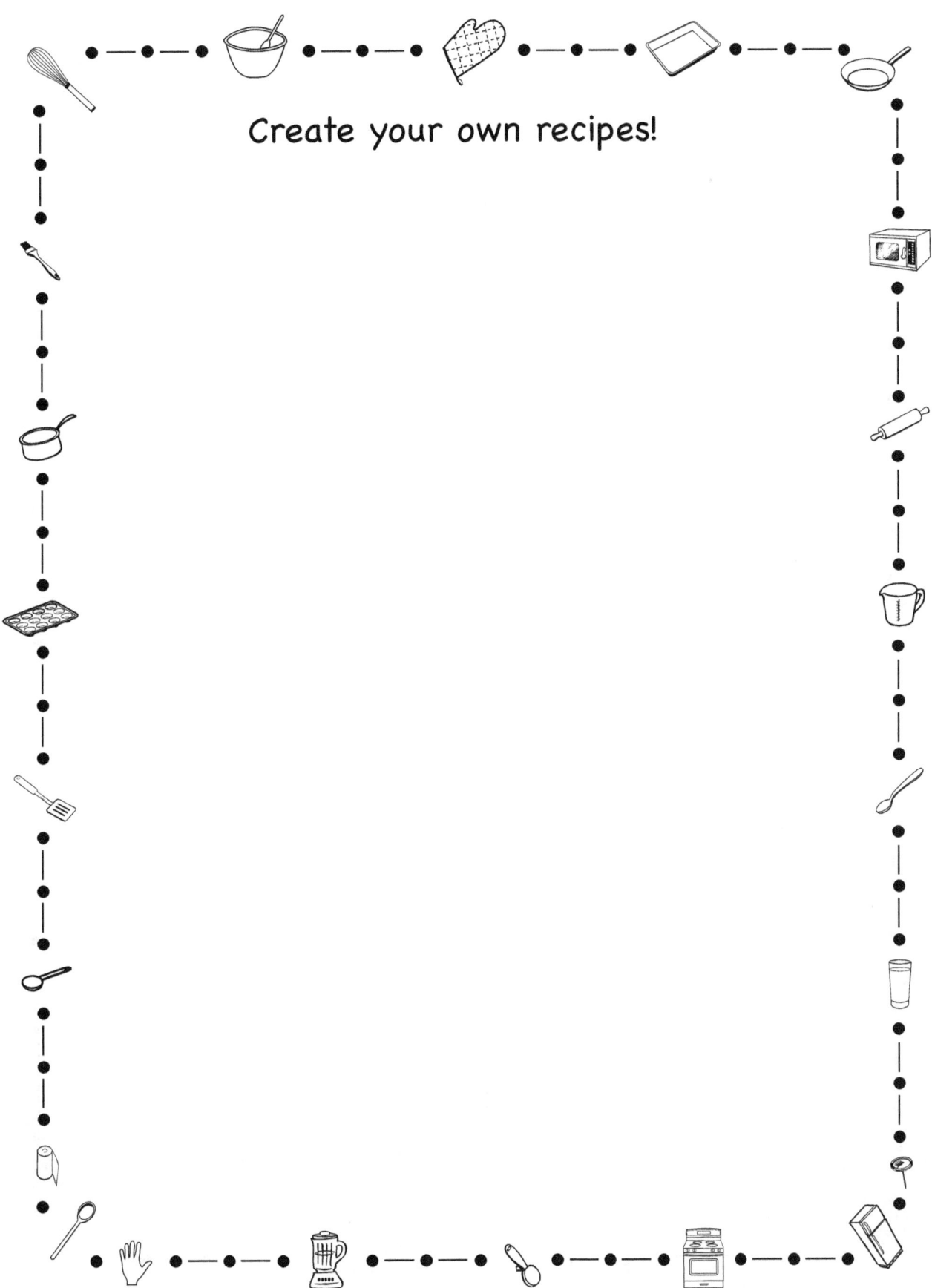

Create your own recipes!

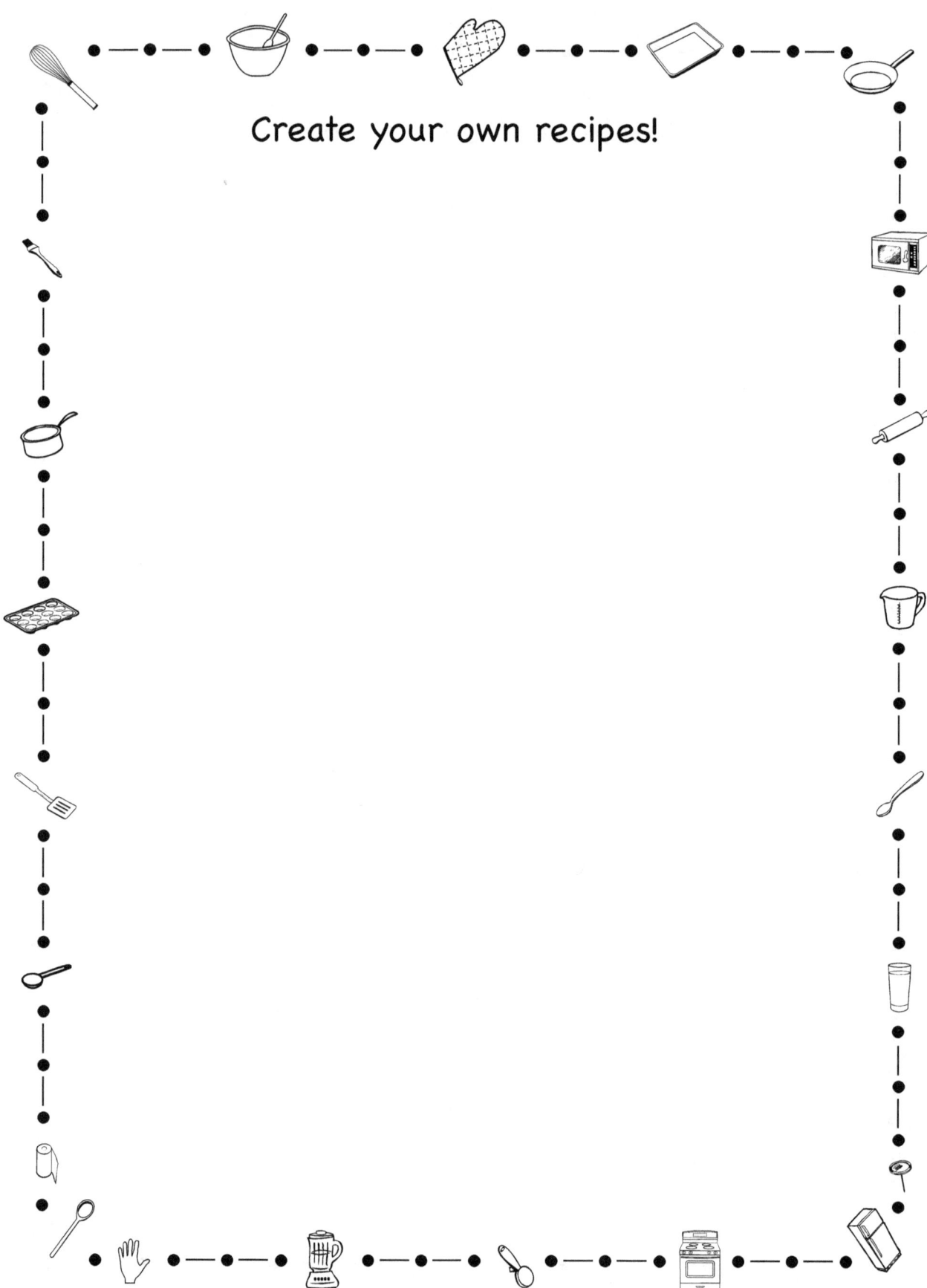

Create your own recipes!

Meet the Alphabet Kitchen Test Cooks!

Thank you to all of the fabulously talented 26 Alphabet Kitchen Test Cooks ages 4–16 from Texas, Oklahoma, Maryland, Ohio, Florida, Pennsylvania, California, Massachusetts, Oregon, Arkansas and Germany!

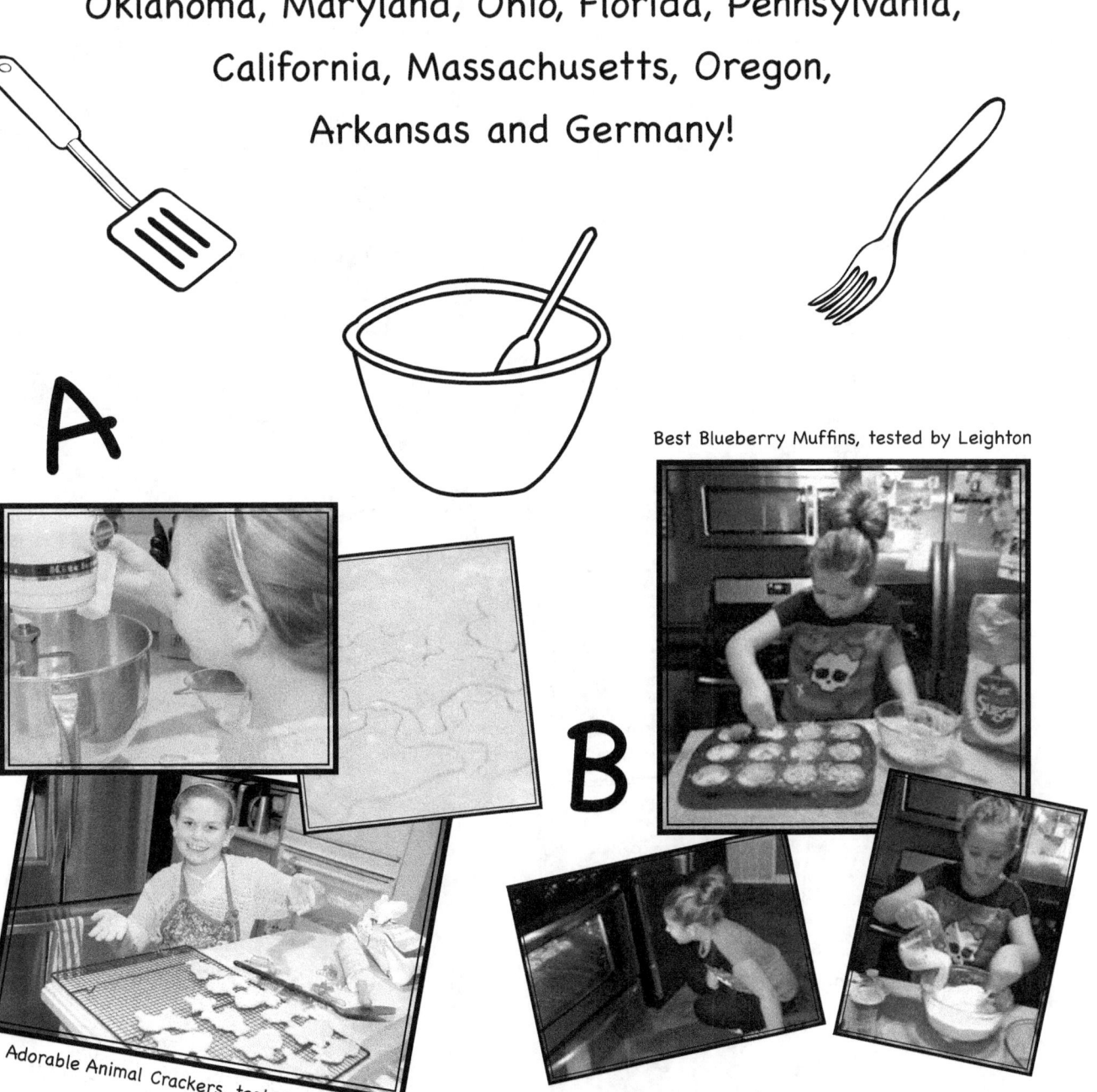

A

Adorable Animal Crackers, tested by Paige

B

Best Blueberry Muffins, tested by Leighton

C — Cool Cherry Dump Cobbler
Tested by Chloe along with her brother, Jack

D — Delightfully Delicious Doughnut Holes
Tested by Callista

E — Easy Extraordinary Egg Casserole
Tested by Cameron

F — Fluffy Fabulous Flapjacks
Tested by Courtney, whose flapjacks won the Grand Prize in a cooking contest!

80

G

H — Horribly Messy Hamburgers, tested by Ashley

Groovy Graham Crackers, tested by Bailey

I

J — Jazzy JELL-O Popcorn Balls

Ice Cream Nanas, tested by Mack

Tested by Luke

K

Krazy Dog Kebobs, tested by Sadler

L

Lucky Cheese Log

Tested by Cooper

M

Tested by Leila

Merry Marshmallow Brownies

N

Nifty Nutty Snowballs

Tested by Chloe

O
Outstanding Orange Drink, tested by Lindsey

P
Pepperoni Pizza Puffs, tested by Khloe

Q
Quick Quiche Cups

Tested by Berghan

R
Tested by Avery

Reece's Rice Krispie Treats

S

Spaghetti in a Skillet, tested by Mr. Greenwood's Gang

T

Tasty French Toast

Tested by Addi

U

Tested by Mason

Upside Down Cupcakes

V

Tested by Audrey

Velvety Velveeta Mac and Cheese

Annette Bridges

Annette Bridges is hoping to empower, encourage, and entertain through the written word. She has published three nonfiction books for women, one coloring storybook for children, and now one youth cookbook. Before writing books, this former public school and homeschool educator spent a decade writing inspirational and light-hearted columns for Texas newspapers, parenting magazines, and spirituality websites. Annette lives on a North Texas cattle ranch with her husband John, mini-dachshund Lady, and lots of cows. Her grown up daughter Jennifer and her mini-dachshund Bella come for a visit often. Lady and Bella are best friends!

You can learn more about Annette and her books and blogs at

www.annettebridges.com

And she invites you to follow her on Facebook, Twitter & Pinterest.

illustration • graphic design • creative solutions

Lesley Vernon is an artist, illustrator, and graphic designer who resides in the Boston area. From a young age, Lesley has loved drawing and doodling, filling the pages of many sketchbooks. She credits an enthusiastic high school art teacher for inspiring her to pursue art more seriously. After earning a bachelor's degree in Studio Art, Lesley has worked in a variety of artistic avenues, including print, web, illustration, and vinyl decals. She loves sharing art with her two young sons Mason and Ryder by coloring, painting, and other hands-on crafts.

You can reach Lesley by email at lesley@lvdesignhouse.com,
or see more of her work on her website at

www.lvdesignhouse.com

Also by Annette Bridges

Lady and Bella
Totally Different, Totally Friends

Lady and Bella
Totally Friends Journal

The Gospel According to Mamma
One mother's philosophy on love,
money, God, aging, decisions,
change, and much more

Be Queen of Your Life
A savvy mom helps daughters command
and rule their lives

Have Lipstick, Will Travel
How to reimagine your life,
purpose & hair color

www.ingramcontent.com/pod-product-compliance
Lightning Source LLC
Chambersburg PA
CBHW080413300426
44113CB00015B/2510